DEADLY *VENOM*

T0002246

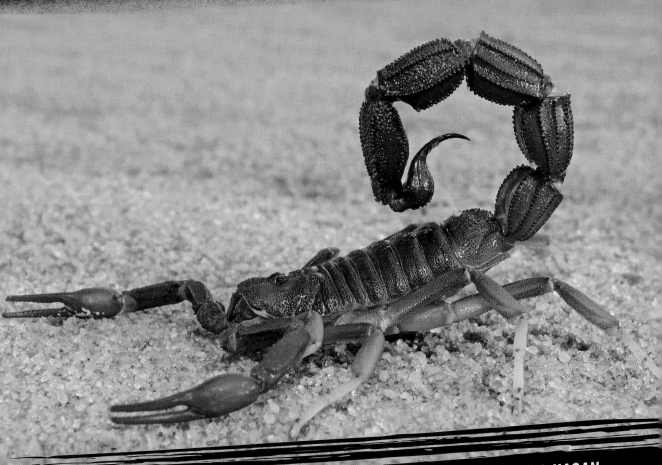

BY VIRGINIA LOH-HAGAN

45TH PARALLEL PRESS

Published in the United States of America by Cherry Lake Publishing Group
Ann Arbor, Michigan
www.cherrylakepublishing.com

Reading Adviser: Beth Walker Gambro, MS Ed., Reading Consultant, Yorkville, IL
Book Designer: Melinda Millward

Photo Credits: Cover: © EcoPrint/Shutterstock; Page 1: © EcoPrint/Shutterstock; Page 5: © EcoPrint/Shutterstock; Page 6: © Kris Wiktor/Shutterstock, © Vaclav Sebek/Shutterstock; Page 7: © reptiles4all/Shutterstock; Page 8: © Evelyn D. Harrison/Shutterstock; Page 10: © NOTE OMG/Shutterstock, © EcoPrint/Shutterstock; Page 11: © Ecophoto/Dreamstime; Page 12: © Vladimir Wrangel/Shutterstock, © Roman Vintonyak/Shutterstock; Page 13: © Jxpfeer/Dreamstime; Page 14: © OneClic/Adobe Stock; Page 16: © Rizik/Shutterstock, © Laura Dts/Shutterstock; Page 17: © Cyhel/Shutterstock; Page 18: © Nuttawut Uttamaharad/Shutterstock, © Paul/Adobe Stock; Page 19: © THEGIFT777/iStockphoto; Page 20: © Henryp982/Shutterstock; Page 22: © Adam Ke/Shutterstock, © Yann hubert/Shutterstock; Page 23: © Wirestock Creators/Shutterstock

Graphic Element Credits: Cover, multiple interior pages: © paprika/Shutterstock, © Silhouette Lover/Shutterstock, © Daria Rosen/Shutterstock, © Wi_Stock/Shutterstock

Library of Congress Cataloging-in-Publication Data

Names: Loh-Hagan, Virginia, author.
Title: Deadly venom / written by Virginia Loh-Hagan.
Description: Ann Arbor, Michigan : Cherry Lake Publishing, [2023] | Series: Wild Wicked Wonderful Express. | Audience: Grades 2-3 | Summary: "Which animals are known for their deadly venom? This book explores the wild, wicked, and wonderful world of venomous animals. Series is developed to aid struggling and reluctant young readers with engaging high-interest content, considerate text, and clear visuals. Includes table of contents, glossary with simplified pronunciations, index, sidebars, and author biographies"—Provided by publisher.
Identifiers: LCCN 2022042687 | ISBN 9781668920725 (paperback) | ISBN 9781668919705 (hardcover) | ISBN 9781668923382 (pdf) | ISBN 9781668922057 (ebook)
Subjects: LCSH: Poisonous animals—Juvenile literature.
Classification: LCC QL100 .L645 2023 | DDC 591.6/5—dc23/eng/20220913
LC record available at httA://lccn.loc.gov/2022042687

Cherry Lake Publishing Group would like to acknowledge the work of the Partnership for 21st Century Learning, a Network of Battelle for Kids. Please visit http://www.battelleforkids.org/networks/p21 for more information.

Printed in the United States of America
Corporate Graphics

About the Author

Dr. Virginia Loh-Hagan is an author, university professor, former classroom teacher, and curriculum designer. She does not like venom. She lives in San Diego with her very tall husband and very naughty dogs.

Table of Contents

Introduction

Animals bite. They sting. They use **venom**. It harms **victims**. Victims are targets of attacks. Venom causes pain. It can make victims not able to move. It can cause death.

Animals inject venom. They do this to protect themselves. They want to **survive**. Survive means to stay alive. They fight **predators**. Predators hunt other animals for food. But venomous animals need to eat. They inject venom into **prey**. Prey are animals hunted for food.

Some animals have extreme venom. Their venom is bigger. Their venom is better. They have the most exciting venom in the animal world!

There are different types of venom.

Gila Monsters

Gila monsters are lizards that make venom. Not many lizards do this. Gila monsters are special. They're the largest U.S. lizards. They're 2 feet (0.6 meters) long. They weigh up to 5 pounds (2.3 kilograms). They're slow much of the time. But they strike quickly.

They bite. Their teeth are sharp. Their teeth slice open skin. They have special saliva **glands**. Glands are organs that release substances.

When a gila monster bites prey, venom flows along grooves in their teeth and into the bite.

Gila monsters were first found in the Gila River basin of Arizona. It's where they get their name!

Gila monster glands make venom. Venom flows into open cuts.

Their venom makes victims sick. Victims feel pain. Their organs get damaged. They get cold sweats. They can't move.

When Animals Attack!

Bees, wasps, and hornets are small. But they kill about 60 people a year in the U.S. They kill more people than sharks, crocodiles, and snakes combined. Some people die from shock because they're **allergic** to stings. Allergic means having a highly sensitive reaction to something. Only female bees and wasps sting. Honey bees can only sting once. Once they sting, they die soon after. Wasps can sting several times. Their stinger doesn't fall off after use. Wasps' stings usually wear off in a day. But some people react very badly. Wasp venom can kill some people. Hornet stings hurt the most. Like wasps, they can sting several times.

Scorpions

Scorpions are related to spiders. They have **pincers**. Pincers are claws. Scorpions have tails. Their tails curve over their backs. The tails have stingers filled with venom.

All scorpions have venom. But only about 25 types of scorpions can kill people.

Scorpions control their stings. They control the venom they release. They can stun. They can kill. Sometimes, they use a little venom. This causes pain. But it doesn't kill. They don't want to waste venom.

Scorpions smell to find food
and to hide from danger.

Stonefish

Stonefish live in the Pacific Ocean. They're dangerous and very venomous.

These fish have 12 to 14 spines. Thick skin covers their spines. Each spine has a venom gland. Their venom causes pain. It causes death.

Stonefish sit at ocean bottoms. They look like stones. Their spines lie flat. They open their spines and sting when other animals come close. This protects them.

Stonefish blend into the ocean floor!

Stonefish have the most venom out of any fish in the entire world!

Stonefish can sting out of water. They can live on the beach. They can be out of water for 24 hours! Sometimes people step on stonefish and are stung. These people need medical treatment right away.

Humans Do What?!?

In Haiti, some people believe in zombies. Zombies are said to be dead people who come back to life. Some people believe voodoo magic brings them back to life. Puffer fish are venomous. Voodoo followers grind up puffer fish. This causes **paralysis**. Paralysis means being unable to move.

Cone Snails

Cone snails are small. They're slow. They can't chase prey. But they have to eat. So they use venom. Their venom is strong.

These snails are dangerous. They've killed more than 30 humans. But their normal prey is worms and small fish.

They have a special tooth. The tooth injects deadly venom. Their attacks take less than a second.

The snails then eat the prey whole. They vomit the scales and bones.

Cone snails can grow to about
6 inches (15.2 centimeters).

Box Jellyfish

Deadly box jellyfish live in Australia. They're also called sea wasps. They're the world's most venomous animals. The venom from one box jellyfish can kill 60 people. It can do this in minutes.

The jellyfish have deadly **tentacles**. Tentacles are flexible arms. The tentacles have millions of stingers. The stingers are like tiny darts. They hold venom.

Box jellyfish venom attacks hearts. It attacks spines. It attacks brains. Victims can't move. Victims can die.

Victims have scars from box jellyfish. People say it's like being branded with red-hot irons.

Unlike other jellyfish, box jellyfish can move themselves through the water.

Some humans have died. Some survived. But they still felt pain for weeks. They have many scars.

Box jellyfish are pale blue. They're clear. They're shaped like boxes. Victims don't feel stings. But the victims do feel the venom.

Did You Know...?

- Some people get bee venom therapy. They want to get stung. They think bee stings help some symptoms of certain diseases.

- Scientists use Gila monster spit. They put the venom in drugs. The drugs help people with memory loss.

- Cone snail venom is used as a painkiller. Scientists think it's 1,000 times more effective than other powerful painkillers.

Stingrays

Stingrays live in warm waters. They have stingers under their tails. They can be more dangerous than sharks.

They bury themselves. They hide in sand. Victims step on them. Stingrays whip their tails around. Their stingers strike.

Pain comes quickly. Stingray venom can be deadly.

Tails help stingrays swim. But their stingers are for protection.

Consider This!

Take a Position! Should we, as humans, be afraid of venomous animals? Why or why not?

Think About It! Animals seem to have different ways to protect themselves. Using venom is one of them. How do humans protect themselves?

Learn More
- **Book:** 2015. Venomous Animals of the World. Baby Professor.
- **Article:** National Geographic Kids - "Scorpion." March 1, 2014: https://kids.nationalgeographic.com/animals/invertebrates/facts/scorpion.

Glossary

allergic (uh-LUR-jik) having a highly sensitive reaction to something

glands (GLANDZ) organs that produce substances used by the body

paralysis (puh-RA-luh-suhs) loss of the ability to move

pincers (PIHN-suhrz) claws

predators (PREH-duh-turz) animals that hunt other animals for food

prey (PRAY) animals hunted for food

survive (sur-VYV) stay alive

tentacles (TEHN-tih-kuhlz) long, flexible arms found on some animals

venom (VEH-nuhm) an injected toxin produced by some animals

victims (VIK-tuhmz) targets of attacks or harm

Index